The Pleasure of the Text

Roland Barthes

The Pleasure of the Text

Translated by Richard Miller

With a Note on the Text
by Richard Howard

HILL AND WANG · NEW YORK
A division of Farrar, Straus and Giroux

Translation and Note on the Text © 1975
by Farrar, Straus and Giroux, Inc.
Originally published in French as *Le Plaisir du texte*
© 1973 by Éditions du Seuil, Paris
All rights reserved
First American edition, 1975
Published in Canada by HarperCollins*CanadaLtd*
Printed in the United States of America
Designed by Karen Watt
Twenty-third printing, 1998

Library of Congress Cataloging-in-Publication Data
Barthes, Roland.
The pleasure of the text.
Translation of Le plaisir du texte.
1. Literature—Aesthetics. I. Title.
PN45.B2813   1975   801'.93   75–4904

A Note on the Text

The French have a distinguishing advantage which Roland Barthes, a Frenchman through and through, has taken, has used, has exploited in his new book about what we do when we enjoy a text; the French have a vocabulary of eroticism, an amorous discourse which smells neither of the laboratory nor of the sewer, which just—attentively, scrupulously—puts the facts. In English, we have either the coarse or the clinical, and by tradition our words for our pleasures, even for the intimate parts of our bodies where we may take those pleasures, come awkwardly when they come at all. So that if we wish to speak of the kind of pleasure we take—the supreme pleasure, say, associated with sexuality at its most abrupt and ruthless pitch—we lack the terms acknowledged and allowed in polite French utterance; we lack *jouissance* and *jouir,* as Barthes uses them here. The nomenclature of active pleasure fails us—that is the "matter" Sterne had in mind when he said they order this matter so much better in France.

Roland Barthes's translator, Richard Miller, has been resourceful, of course, and he has come up with the readiest plausibility by translating *jouissance* (for the most part: Barthes himself declares the choice between pleasure and the more ravaging term to be precarious, revocable, the discourse incomplete) as "bliss"; but of course he cannot come up with "coming," which precisely translates what the original text can afford. The Bible they translated calls it "knowing" while the Stuarts called it "dying," the Victorians called it "spending," and we call it "coming"; a hard look at the horizon of our literary culture suggests that it will not be long before we come to a new word for orgasm proper—we shall call it "being."

Roland Barthes, in any case, calls it *jouissance,* as his own literary culture entitles him to do, and he associates his *theory of the text,* in this new book, with what has been a little neglected in his own and other (French) studies of what we may take, what we may have, when we read: the pleasure of the text. Pleasure is a state, of course, bliss *(jouissance)* an action, and both of them, in our culture, are held to be unspeakable, beyond words. Here, for example, is Willa Cather, a writer Barthes has never heard of, putting in a plea of *nolo contendere,* which is, for all its insufferable air of customary infallibility, no more than symptomatic:

> The qualities of a first-rate writer cannot be defined, but only experienced. It is just the thing in him which escapes analysis that makes him first-rate. One can catalogue all the qualities that he shares with other writers, but the thing that is his very own, his timbre, this cannot be defined or explained any more than the quality of a beautiful speaking voice can be.

In the puritanism of our expressivity, what can be said is taken—is likely—to be no longer experienced, certainly no longer enjoyed.

Yet Barthes has found, for all Cather's strictures, a way to *speak pleasure,* a way which leads him to abandon the systematics of earlier studies (he has found this way before: this new book is to *S/Z* as his essay on Japan, *L'Empire des Signes,* is to *Système de la Mode*: a writer's aphrodisiac); his way is to give himself away—literally, to confess, to speak with all the entranced conviction of a man in the dock: to give himself up to an evidently random succession of fragments: facets, aphorisms, touches and shoves, nudges, elbowings, bubbles, trial balloons, "phylacteries," he calls them, of an invisible design—the design is the simple staging of the question "What do we enjoy in the text?" The design is not quite invisible, perhaps, for it obeys the most arbitrary (and apparent) of orders, the alphabetical, which governs Barthes's series of *proses** in such a fashion that we feel held somewhere between the high-handed and the under-handed in the aspiration to catch pleasure out, the effort to catch up with bliss. Like filings which gather to form a figure in a magnetic field, the parts and pieces here do come together, determined to affirm the pleasure we must take in our reading as against the indifference of (mere) knowledge, determined to instance our ecstasy, our bliss in the text against the prudery of ideological analysis, so that perhaps for the first time in the history of criticism we have not only a poetics of reading—that, I think, is what

* In the Church, a *prose* or *sequence* is a "rhythm" sung after the epistle, and so called because not in any regular meter.

vii

Barthes has managed so marvelously to constitute in *S/Z*—but a much more difficult (because supposedly inexpressible, apparently ineffable) achievement, an *erotics of reading.*

RICHARD HOWARD

Contents

ix

Atque metum tantum concepit tunc mea mater
Ut paretet geminos, meque metumque simul.

—Hobbes

The Pleasure
of the Text

THE PLEASURE OF THE TEXT: like Bacon's simulator, it can say: *never apologize, never explain.* It never denies anything: "I shall look away, that will henceforth be my sole negation."

~ ~ ~

Imagine someone (a kind of Monsieur Teste in reverse) who abolishes within himself all barriers, all classes, all exclusions, not by syncretism but by simple discard of that old specter: *logical contradiction;* who mixes every language, even those said to be incompatible; who silently accepts every charge of illogicality, of incongruity; who remains passive in the face of Socratic irony (leading the interlocutor to the supreme disgrace: *self-contradiction*) and legal terrorism (how much penal evidence is based on a psychology of consistency!). Such a man would be the mockery of our society: court, school, asylum, polite conversation would cast him out: who endures contradiction without shame? Now this anti-hero exists: he is the reader of the text at the moment he takes his pleasure. Thus the Biblical myth is reversed, the confusion of tongues is no longer a punishment, the subject gains access to bliss by the cohabitation of languages *working side by side:* the text of pleasure is a sanctioned Babel.

(*Pleasure/Bliss:* terminologically, there is always a vacillation—I stumble, I err. In any case, there will always be a margin of indecision; the distinction will not be the source of absolute classifications, the paradigm will falter, the meaning will be precarious, revocable, reversible, the discourse incomplete.)

~ ~ ~

If I read this sentence, this story, or this word with pleasure, it is because they were written in pleasure (such pleasure does not contradict the writer's complaints). But the opposite? Does writing in pleasure guarantee—guarantee me, the writer—my reader's pleasure? Not at all. I must seek out this reader (must "cruise" him) *without knowing where he is.* A site of bliss is then created. It is not the reader's "person" that is necessary to me, it is this site: the possibility of a dialectics of desire, of an *unpredictability* of bliss: the bets are not placed, there can still be a game.

I am offered a text. This text bores me. It might be said to *prattle.* The prattle of the text is merely that foam of language which forms by the effect of a simple need of writing. Here we are not dealing with perversion but with demand. The writer of this text employs an unweaned language: imperative, automatic, unaffectionate, a minor disaster of static (those milky phonemes which the remarkable Jesuit, van Ginnekin, posited between writing and language): these are the motions of ungratified sucking, of an undifferentiated orality, intersecting the orality which produces the pleasures of gastrosophy and of language. You address yourself to me so that I may read you, but I am nothing to you except this address; in your eyes, I am the substitute for nothing, for no figure (hardly that of the mother); for you I am neither a body nor even an object (and I couldn't care less: I am not the one whose soul demands recognition), but merely a field, a vessel for expansion. It can be said that after all you have written this text quite apart from bliss; and this prattling text is then a frigid text, as any demand is frigid until desire, until neurosis forms in it.

Neurosis is a makeshift: not with regard to "health" but with regard to the "impossible" Bataille speaks of ("Neurosis is the fearful apprehension of an ultimate impossible," etc.); but this makeshift is the only one that allows for writing (and reading). So we arrive at this paradox: the texts, like those by Bataille—or by others—which written against neurosis, from the center of madness, contain within themselves, *if they want to be read,* that bit of neurosis necessary to the seduction of their readers: these terrible texts are *all the same* flirtatious texts.

Thus every writer's motto reads: *mad I cannot be, sane I do not deign to be, neurotic I am.*

The text you write must prove to me *that it desires me.* This proof exists: it is writing. Writing is: the science of the various blisses of language, its Kama Sutra (this science has but one treatise: writing itself).

~ ~ ~

Sade: the pleasure of reading him clearly proceeds from certain breaks (or certain collisions): antipathetic codes (the noble and the trivial, for example) come into contact; pompous and ridiculous neologisms are created; pornographic messages are embodied in sentences so pure they might be used as grammatical models. As textual theory has it: the language is redistributed. Now, *such redistribution is always achieved by cutting.* Two edges are created: an obedient, conformist, plagiarizing edge (the language is to be copied in its canonical state, as it has been established by schooling, good usage, literature, culture), and *another edge,* mobile, blank (ready to assume any contours), which is never anything but the site of its effect: the place where the death of language is glimpsed. These two edges, *the compromise they bring about,* are necessary. Neither culture nor its destruction is erotic; it is the seam between them, the fault, the flaw, which becomes so. The pleasure of the text is like that untenable, impossible, purely *novelistic* instant so relished by Sade's libertine when he manages to be hanged and then to cut the rope at the very moment of his orgasm, his bliss.

Whence, perhaps, a means of evaluating the works of our modernity: their value would proceed from their duplicity. By which it must be understood that they always have two edges. The subversive edge may seem privileged because it is the edge of violence; but it is not violence which affects pleasure, nor is it destruction which interests it; what pleasure wants is the site of a loss, the seam, the cut, the deflation, the *dissolve* which seizes the subject in the midst of bliss. Culture thus recurs as an edge: in no matter what form.

Especially, of course (here is where the edge will be clearest), in the form of a pure materiality: the language, its lexicon, its metrics, its prosody. In Philippe Sollers's *Lois,* everything is attacked, dismantled: ideological structures, intellectual solidarities, the propriety of idioms, and even the sacred armature of syntax (subject/predicate): the text no longer has the sentence for its model; often it is a powerful gush of words, a ribbon of infra-language. Yet it all collides with another edge: that of (decasyllabic) meter, of assonance, of plausible neologisms, of prosodic rhythms, of (quoted) truisms. The dismantling of language is intersected by political assertion, is *edged* by the age-old culture of the signifier.

In Severo Sarduy's *Cobra*, the alternation is that of two pleasures *in a state of competition;* the other edge is the other delight: *more, more, still more!* one more word, one more celebration. Language reconstructs itself *elsewhere* under the teeming flux of every kind of linguistic pleasure. Where is this elsewhere? In the paradise of words. *Cobra* is in fact a paradisiac text, utopian (without site), a heterology by plenitude: all the signifiers are here and each scores a bull's-eye; the author (the reader) seems to say to them: *I love you all* (words, phrases, sentences, adjectives, discontinuities: pell-mell: signs and mirages of objects which they represent); a kind of Franciscanism invites all words to perch, to flock, to fly off again: a marbled, iridescent text; we are gorged with language, like children who are never refused anything or scolded for anything or, even worse, "permitted" anything. *Cobra* is the pledge of continuous jubilation, the moment when by its very excess verbal pleasure chokes and reels into bliss.

Flaubert: a way of cutting, of perforating discourse *without rendering it meaningless.*

Of course, rhetoric recognizes discontinuities in construction (anacoluthons) and in subordination (asyndetons); but with Flaubert, for the first time, discontinuity is no longer exceptional, sporadic, brilliant, set in the base matter of common utterance: there is no longer a language *on the other side* of these figures (which means, in another sense: there is no longer anything but language); a generalized asyndeton seizes the entire utterance, so that this very readable discourse is *underhandedly* one of the craziest imaginable: all the logical small change is in the interstices.

This is a very subtle and nearly untenable status for discourse: narrativity is dismantled yet the story is still readable: never have the two edges of the seam been clearer and more tenuous, never has pleasure been better offered to the reader—if at least he appreciates controlled discontinuities, faked conformities, and indirect destructions. In addition to the success which can here be attributed to an author, there is also, here, a pleasure of performance: the feat is to sustain the *mimesis* of language (language imitating itself), the source of immense pleasures, in a fashion so *radically* ambiguous (ambiguous to the root) that the text never succumbs to the good conscience (and bad faith) of parody (of castrating laughter, of "the comical that makes us laugh").

Is not the most erotic portion of a body *where the garment gapes?* In perversion (which is the realm of textual

9

pleasure) there are no "erogenous zones" (a foolish expression, besides); it is intermittence, as psychoanalysis has so rightly stated, which is erotic: the intermittence of skin flashing between two articles of clothing (trousers and sweater), between two edges (the open-necked shirt, the glove and the sleeve); it is this flash itself which seduces, or rather: the staging of an appearance-as-disappearance.

The pleasure of the text is not the pleasure of the corporeal striptease or of narrative suspense. In these cases, there is no tear, no edges: a gradual unveiling: the entire excitation takes refuge in the *hope* of seeing the sexual organ (schoolboy's dream) or in knowing the end of the story (novelistic satisfaction). Paradoxically (since it is mass-consumed), this is a far more intellectual pleasure than the other: an Oedipal pleasure (to denude, to know, to learn the origin and the end), if it is true that every narrative (every unveiling of the truth) is a staging of the (absent, hidden, or hypostatized) father—which would explain the solidarity of narrative forms, of family structures, and of prohibitions of nudity, all collected in our culture in the myth of Noah's sons covering his nakedness.

Yet the most classical narrative (a novel by Zola or Balzac or Dickens or Tolstoy) bears within it a sort of diluted tmesis: we do not read everything with the same intensity of reading; a rhythm is established, casual, unconcerned with the *integrity* of the text; our very avidity for knowledge impels us to skim or to skip certain passages (anticipated as "boring") in order to get more quickly to the warmer parts of the anecdote (which are always its articulations: whatever furthers the solution of the riddle, the revelation of fate): we boldly skip (no one is watching) descriptions, explanations, analyses, conversations; doing so, we resemble a spectator in a nightclub who climbs onto the stage and speeds up the dancer's striptease, tearing off her clothing, *but in the same order*, that is: on the one hand respecting and on the other hastening the episodes of the ritual (like a priest *gulping down* his Mass). Tmesis, source or figure of pleasure, here confronts two prosaic edges with one another; it sets what is useful to a knowledge of the secret against what is useless to such knowledge; tmesis is a seam or flaw resulting from a simple principle of functionality; it does not occur at the level of the structure of languages but only at the moment of their consumption; the author cannot predict tmesis: he cannot choose to write *what will not be read*. And yet, it is the very rhythm of what is read and what is not read that creates the pleasure of the great narratives: has anyone ever read Proust, Balzac, *War and Peace*, word for word? (Proust's good fortune: from one reading to the next, we never skip the same passages.)

Thus, what I enjoy in a narrative is not directly its content or even its structure, but rather the abrasions I impose upon the fine surface: I read on, I skip, I look up, I dip in again. Which has nothing to do with the deep laceration the text of bliss inflicts upon language itself, and not upon the simple temporality of its reading.

Whence two systems of reading: one goes straight to the articulations of the anecdote, it considers the extent of the text, ignores the play of language (if I read Jules Verne, I go fast: I lose discourse, and yet my reading is not hampered by any verbal *loss*—in the speleological sense of that word); the other reading skips nothing; it weighs, it sticks to the text, it reads, so to speak, with application and transport, grasps at every point in the text the asyndeton which cuts the various languages—and not the anecdote: it is not (logical) extension that captivates it, the winnowing out of truths, but the layering of significance; as in the children's game of topping hands, the excitement comes not from a processive haste but from a kind of vertical din (the verticality of language and of its destruction); it is at the moment when each (different) hand skips over the next (and not one *after* the other) that the hole, the gap, is created and carries off the subject of the game—the subject of the text. Now paradoxically (so strong is the belief that one need merely *go fast* in order not to be bored), this second, *applied* reading (in the real sense of the word "application") is the one suited to the modern text, the limit-text. Read slowly, read *all* of a novel by Zola, and the book will drop from your hands; read fast, in snatches, some modern text, and it becomes opaque, inaccessible to your pleasure: you want something to happen and nothing does, for *what happens to the language does not happen to the discourse:* what "happens," what "goes away," the seam of the two edges, the interstice of bliss, occurs in the volume of the languages, in the uttering, not in the sequence of utterances: not to devour, to gobble, but to graze, to browse scrupulously, to rediscover—in order to read today's writers—the leisure of bygone readings: to be *aristocratic* readers.

~ ~ ~

If I agree to judge a text according to pleasure, I cannot go on to say: this one is good, that bad. No awards, no "critique," for this always implies a tactical aim, a social usage, and frequently an extenuating image-reservoir. I cannot apportion, imagine that the text is perfectible, ready to enter into a play of normative predicates: it is too much *this,* not enough *that;* the text (the same is true of the singing voice) can wring from me only this judgment, in no way adjectival: *that's it!* And further still: *that's it for me!* This "for me" is neither subjective nor existential, but Nietzschean (". . . basically, it is always the same question: What is it *for me?* . . .").

The *brio* of the text (without which, after all, there is no text) is its *will to bliss:* just where it exceeds demand, transcends prattle, and whereby it attempts to overflow, to break through the constraint of adjectives—which are those doors of language through which the ideological and the imaginary come flowing in.

~ ~ ~

Text of pleasure: the text that contents, fills, grants euphoria; the text that comes from culture and does not break with it, is linked to a *comfortable* practice of reading. Text of bliss: the text that imposes a state of loss, the text that discomforts (perhaps to the point of a certain boredom), unsettles the reader's historical, cultural, psychological assumptions, the consistency of his tastes, values, memories, brings to a crisis his relation with language.

Now the subject who keeps the two texts in his field and in his hands the reins of pleasure and bliss is an anachronic subject, for he simultaneously and contradictorily participates in the profound hedonism of all culture (which permeates him quietly under cover of an *art de vivre* shared by the old books) and in the destruction of that culture: he enjoys the consistency of his selfhood (that is his pleasure) and seeks its loss (that is his bliss). He is a subject split twice over, doubly perverse.

~ ~ ~

Society of the Friends of the Text: its members would have nothing in common (for there is no necessary agreement on the texts of pleasure) but their enemies:

14

fools of all kinds, who decree foreclosure of the text and of its pleasure, either by cultural conformism or by intransigent rationalism (suspecting a "mystique" of literature) or by political moralism or by criticism of the signifier or by stupid pragmatism or by snide vacuity or by destruction of the discourse, loss of verbal desire. Such a society would have no site, could function only in total atopia; yet it would be a kind of phalanstery, for in it contradictions would be acknowledged (and the risks of ideological imposture thereby restricted), difference would be observed, and conflict rendered insignificant (being unproductive of pleasure).

"Let difference surreptitiously replace conflict." Difference is not what makes or sweetens conflict: it is achieved over and above conflict, it is *beyond and alongside* conflict. Conflict is nothing but the moral state of difference; whenever (and this is becoming frequent) conflict is not tactical (aimed at transforming a real situation), one can distinguish in it the failure-to-attain-bliss, the debacle of a perversion crushed by its own code and no longer able to invent itself: conflict is always coded, aggression is merely the most worn-out of languages. Forgoing violence, I forgo the code itself (in Sade's texts, outside all codes because they continually invent their own, appropriate only to themselves, there are no conflicts: only triumphs). I love the text because for me it is that rare locus of language from which any "scene" (in the household, conjugal sense of the term), any logomachy is absent. The text is never a "dialogue": no risk of feint, of aggression, of blackmail, no rivalry of ideolects; the text establishes a sort of islet within the human—the common—relation, manifests the asocial nature of pleasure (only leisure is social), grants a glimpse of the scandalous truth about bliss: that it may well be, once the image-reservoir of speech is abolished, *neuter*.

~ ~ ~

On the stage of the text, no footlights: there is not, behind the text, someone active (the writer) and out front someone passive (the reader); there is not a subject and an object. The text supersedes grammatical attitudes: it is the undifferentiated eye which an excessive author (Angelus Silesius) describes: "The eye by which I see God is the same eye by which He sees me."

Apparently Arab scholars, when speaking of the text, use this admirable expression: *the certain body*. What body? We have several of them; the body of anatomists and physiologists, the one science sees or discusses: this is the text of grammarians, critics, commentators, philologists (the pheno-text). But we also have a body of bliss consisting solely of erotic relations, utterly distinct from the first body: it is another contour, another nomination; thus with the text: it is no more than the open list of the fires of language (those living fires, intermittent lights, wandering features strewn in the text like seeds and which for us advantageously replace the *"semina aeternitatis,"* the *"zopyra,"* the common notions, the fundamental assumptions of ancient philosophy). Does the text have human form, is it a figure, an anagram of the body? Yes, but of our erotic body. The pleasure of the text is irreducible to physiological need.

The pleasure of the text is that moment when my body pursues its own ideas—for my body does not have the same ideas I do.

~ ~ ~

How can we take pleasure in a *reported* pleasure (boredom of all narratives of dreams, of parties)? How can we read criticism? Only one way: since I am here a second-degree reader, I must shift my position: instead of agreeing to be the confidant of this critical pleasure—a sure way to miss it—I can make myself its voyeur: I observe clandestinely the pleasure of others, I enter perversion; the commentary then becomes in my eyes a text, a fiction, a fissured envelope. The writer's perversity (his pleasure in writing is *without function*), the doubled, the trebled, the infinite perversity of the critic and of his reader.

A text on pleasure cannot be anything but *short* (as we say: *is that all? It's a bit short*); since pleasure can only be spoken through the indirection of a demand (I have a *right* to pleasure), we cannot get beyond an abridged, two-tense dialectics: the tense of *doxa,* opinion, and the tense of *paradoxa,* dispute. A third term is missing, besides pleasure and its censure. This term is postponed to later, and so long as we cling to the very name of "pleasure," every text on pleasure will be nothing but dilatory; it will be an introduction to what will never be written. Like those productions of contemporary art which exhaust their necessity as soon as they have been seen (since to see them is immediately to understand to what destructive purpose they are exhibited: they no longer contain any contemplative or delectative duration), such an introduction can only repeat itself—without ever introducing anything.

~ ~ ~

The pleasure of the text is not necessarily of a triumphant, heroic, muscular type. No need to throw out one's chest. My pleasure can very well take the form of a drift. *Drifting* occurs whenever *I do not respect the whole,* and whenever, by dint of seeming driven about by language's illusions, seductions, and intimidations, like a cork on the waves, I remain motionless, pivoting on the *intractable* bliss that binds me to the text (to the world). Drifting occurs whenever social language, the sociolect, *fails me* (as we say: *my courage fails me*). Thus another name for drifting would be: *the Intractable*—or perhaps even: Stupidity.

However, if one were to manage it, the very utterance of drifting today would be a suicidal discourse.

~ ~ ~

Pleasure of the text, text of pleasure: these expressions are ambiguous because French has no word that simultaneously covers pleasure (contentment) and bliss (rapture). Therefore, "pleasure" here (and without our being able to anticipate) sometimes extends to bliss, sometimes is opposed to it. But I must accommodate myself to this ambiguity; for on the one hand I need a general "pleasure" whenever I must refer to an excess of the text, to what in it exceeds any (social) function and any (structural) functioning; and on the other hand I need a particular "pleasure," a simple part of Pleasure as a whole, whenever I need to distinguish euphoria, fulfillment, comfort (the feeling of repletion when culture penetrates freely), from shock, disturbance, even loss, which are proper to ecstasy, to bliss. I cannot avoid this ambiguity because I cannot cleanse the word "pleasure" of meanings I occasionally do not want: I cannot avoid the fact that in French "pleasure" refers both to a generality *("pleasure principle")* and to a miniaturization *("Fools are put on earth for our minor pleasures").* Thus I must allow the utterance of my text to proceed in contradiction.

Is pleasure only a minor bliss? Is bliss nothing but extreme pleasure? Is pleasure only a weakened, conformist bliss—a bliss deflected through a pattern of conciliations? Is bliss merely a brutal, immediate (without mediation) pleasure? On the answer (yes or no) depends the way in which we shall write the history of our modernity. For if I say that between pleasure and bliss there is only a difference of degree, I am also saying that the history is a pacified one: the text of bliss is merely the logical, organic, historical development of the text of pleasure; the avant-garde is never anything but the progressive, emancipated form of past culture: today emerges from yesterday, Robbe-Grillet is already in Flaubert, Sollers in Rabelais, all of Nicolas de Stael in two square centimeters of Cézanne. But if I believe on the contrary that pleasure and bliss are parallel forces, that they cannot meet, and that between them there is more than a struggle: an *incommunication,* then I must certainly believe that history, our history, is not peaceable and perhaps not even intelligent, that the text of bliss always rises out of it like a scandal (an irregularity), that it is always the trace of a cut, of an assertion (and not of a flowering), and that the subject of this history (this historical subject that I am among others), far from being possibly pacified by combining my taste for works of the past with my advocacy of modern works in a fine dialectical movement of synthesis—this subject is never anything but a "living contradiction": a split subject, who simultaneously enjoys, through the text, the consistency of his selfhood and its collapse, its fall.

Here moreover, drawn from psychoanalysis, is an indirect way of establishing the opposition between the text of pleasure and the text of bliss: pleasure can be expressed in words, bliss cannot.

Bliss is unspeakable, inter-dicted. I refer to Lacan ("What one must bear in mind is that bliss is forbidden to the speaker, as such, or else that it cannot be spoken except between the lines . . .") and to Leclaire (". . . Whoever speaks, by speaking denies bliss, or correlatively, whoever experiences bliss causes the letter— and all possible speech—to collapse in the absolute degree of the annihilation he is celebrating").

The writer of pleasure (and his reader) accepts the letter; renouncing bliss, he has the right and the power to express it: the letter is his pleasure; he is obsessed by it, as are all those who love language (and not speech), logo-philes, authors, letter writers, linguists: about texts of pleasure, therefore, it is possible to speak (no argument with the annihilation of bliss): *criticism always deals with the texts of pleasure, never the texts of bliss:* Flaubert, Proust, Stendhal are discussed inexhaustibly; thus criticism speaks the futile bliss of the tutor text, its *past or future* bliss: *you are about to read, I have read:* criticism is always historical or prospective: the constatory present, the *presentation* of bliss, is forbidden it; its preferred material is thus culture, which is everything in us except our present.

With the writer of bliss (and his reader) begins the untenable text, the impossible text. This text is outside pleasure, outside criticism, *unless it is reached through another text of bliss:* you cannot speak "on" such a text, you can only speak "in" it, *in its fashion,* enter into a desperate plagiarism, hysterically affirm the void of bliss (and no longer obsessively repeat the letter of pleasure).

~ ~ ~

An entire minor mythology would have us believe that pleasure (and singularly the pleasure of the text) is a rightist notion. On the right, with the same movement, everything abstract, boring, political, is shoved over to the left and pleasure is kept for oneself: welcome to our side, you who are finally coming to the pleasure of literature! And on the left, because of morality (forgetting Marx's and Brecht's cigars), one suspects and disdains any "residue of hedonism." On the right, pleasure is championed *against* intellectuality, the clerisy: the old reactionary myth of heart against head, sensation against reasoning, (warm) "life" against (cold) "abstraction": must not the artist, according to Debussy's sinister precept, *"humbly seek to give pleasure"?* On the left, knowledge, method,

commitment, combat, are drawn up against "mere delecta-
tion" (and yet: what if knowledge itself were *delicious?*).
On both sides, this peculiar idea that pleasure is *simple,*
which is why it is championed or disdained. Pleasure,
however, is not an *element* of the text, it is not a naïve
residue; it does not depend on a logic of understanding
and on sensation; it is a drift, something both revolution-
ary and asocial, and it cannot be taken over by any
collectivity, any mentality, any ideolect. Something *neuter?*
It is obvious that the pleasure of the text is scandalous: not
because it is immoral but because it is *atopic.*

~ ~ ~

Why, in a text, all this verbal display? Does luxury of
language belong with excessive wealth, wasteful expendi-
ture, total loss? Does a great work of pleasure (Proust's,
for example) participate in the same economy as the
pyramids of Egypt? Is today's writer the residual substitute
for the beggar, the monk, the bonze: unproductive, but
nevertheless provided for? Analogous to the Buddhist
sangha, is the literary community, whatever alibi it uses,
supported by a mercantile society, not for what the writer
produces (he produces nothing), but for what he con-
sumes? Superfluous, but certainly not useless?
    Our modernity makes a constant effort to defeat the
exchange: it tries to resist the market for works (by
excluding itself from mass communication), the sign (by
exemption from meaning, by madness), sanctioned sexual-

ity (by perversion, which shields bliss from the finality of reproduction). And even so, modernity can do nothing: the exchange recuperates everything, acclimating what appears to deny it: it seizes upon the text, puts it in the circuit of useless but legal expenditures: and behold, the text is back in a collective economy (even if only psychological): it is the text's very uselessness that is useful, as a potlatch. In other words, society lives according to a cleavage: here a sublime, disinterested text, there a mercantile object, whose value is . . . the gratuitousness of this object. But society has no notion of this split: *it is ignorant of its own perversion.* "The two litigants take their share: impulse is entitled to its satisfaction, reality receives the respect which is its due. *But,*" Freud adds, *"nothing is gratuitous except death, as everyone knows."* For the text, nothing is gratuitous except its own destruction: not to write, not to write again, except to be eternally recuperated.

~ ~ ~

To be with the one I love and to think of something else: this is how I have my best ideas, how I best invent what is necessary to my work. Likewise for the text: it produces, in me, the best pleasure if it manages to make itself heard indirectly; if, reading it, I am led to look up often, to listen to something else. I am not necessarily *captivated* by the text of pleasure; it can be an act that is slight, complex, tenuous, almost scatterbrained: a sudden movement of the head like a bird who understands nothing of what we hear, who hears what we do not understand.

~ ~ ~

Emotion: why should it be antipathetic to bliss (I was wrong when I used to see it wholly on the side of sentimentality, of moral illusion)? It is a disturbance, a bordering on collapse: something perverse, under respectable appearances; emotion is even, perhaps, the slyest of losses, for it contradicts the general rule that would assign bliss a fixed form: strong, violent, crude: something inevitably muscular, strained, phallic. Against the general rule: *never allow oneself to be deluded by* the image *of bliss;* agree to recognize bliss wherever a disturbance occurs in amatory adjustment (premature, delayed, etc.): passionate love as bliss? Bliss as wisdom (when it manages to understand itself *outside its own prejudices*)?

~ ~ ~

It can't be helped: boredom is not simple. We do not escape boredom (with a work, a text) with a gesture of impatience or rejection. Just as the pleasure of the text supposes a whole indirect production, so boredom cannot presume it is entitled to any spontaneity: there is no *sincere* boredom: if the prattle-text bores me personally, it is because in reality I do not like the demand. But what if I did like it (if I had some maternal appetite)? Boredom is not far from bliss: it is bliss seen from the shores of pleasure.

~ ~ ~

The more a story is told in a proper, well-spoken, straightforward way, in an even tone, the easier it is to reverse it, to blacken it, to read it inside out (Mme de Ségur read by Sade). This reversal, being a pure production, wonderfully develops the pleasure of the text.

~ ~ ~

In *Bouvard and Pécuchet*, I read this sentence, which gives me pleasure: "Cloths, sheets, napkins were hanging vertically, attached by wooden clothespins to taut lines." Here I enjoy an excess of precision, a kind of maniacal exactitude of language, a descriptive madness (encountered in texts by Robbe-Grillet). We are faced with this paradox: literary language disturbed, exceeded, *ignored,* exactly insofar as it accommodates itself to "pure" language, to essential language, to the grammarian's language (this language, of course, is only a notion). The exactitude in question is not the result of taking greater pains, it is not a rhetorical increment in value, as though things were *increasingly well* described—but of a change of code: the (remote) model of the description is no longer oratorical

26

discourse (nothing at all is being "painted"), but a kind of lexicographical artifact.

~ ~ ~

The text is a fetish object, and *this fetish desires me.* The text chooses me, by a whole disposition of invisible screens, selective baffles: vocabulary, references, readability, etc.; and, lost in the midst of a text (not *behind* it, like a *deus ex machina*) there is always the other, the author. As institution, the author is dead: his civil status, his biographical person have disappeared; dispossessed, they no longer exercise over his work the formidable paternity whose account literary history, teaching, and public opinion had the responsibility of establishing and renewing; but in the text, in a way, *I desire* the author: I need his figure (which is neither his representation nor his projection), as he needs mine (except to "prattle").

~ ~ ~

Ideological systems are fictions (Bacon would have said *stage ghosts*), novels—but classical novels, packed with plots, crises, good and evil characters (the *novelistic* is another thing entirely: a simple unstructured contour, a dissemination of forms, *maya*). Every fiction is supported by a social jargon, a sociolect, with which it identifies: fiction is that degree of consistency a language attains when it has *jelled* exceptionally and finds a sacerdotal class (priests, intellectuals, artists) to speak it generally and to circulate it.

". . . Each people has over it just such a heaven of mathematically distributed concepts, and, when truth is required, it understands that henceforth any conceptual god can be sought nowhere but in *its* sphere" (Nietzsche): we are all caught up in the truth of languages, that is, in their regionality, drawn into the formidable rivalry which controls their proximity. For each jargon (each fiction) fights for hegemony; if power is on its side, it spreads everywhere in the general and daily occurrences of social life, it becomes *doxa,* nature: this is the supposedly apolitical jargon of politicians, of agents of the State, of the media, of conversation; but even out of power, even when power is against it, the rivalry is reborn, the jargons split and struggle among themselves. A ruthless *topic* rules the life of language; language always comes from some place, it is a warrior *topos.*

He used to think of the world of language (the logosphere) as a vast and perpetual conflict of paranoias. The only survivors are the systems (fictions, jargons) inventive enough to produce a final figure, the one which brands the adversary with a half-scientific, half-ethical name, a kind of turnstile that permits us simultaneously to describe, to explain, to condemn, to reject, to recuperate the enemy, in a word: *to make him pay.* So it is, among

28

others, with certain vulgates: with the Marxist jargon, for which all opposition is an opposition of class; with the psychoanalytic jargon, for which all repudiation is avowal; with the Christian jargon, for which all denial is seeking, etc. He was astonished that the language of capitalist power does not constitute, at first glance, such a systematic figure (other than of the basest kind, opponents never being called anything but "rabid," "brainwashed," etc.); then he realized that the (thereby much higher) pressure of capitalist language is not paranoid, systematic, argumentative, articulated: it is an implacable stickiness, a *doxa*, a kind of unconscious: in short, the essence of ideology.

To keep these spoken systems from disturbing or embarrassing us, there is no other solution than to inhabit one of them. Or else: *and me, me, what am I doing in all that?*

The text itself is atopic, if not in its consumption at least in its production. It is not a jargon, a fiction, in it the system is overcome, undone (this overcoming, this defection, is signification). From this atopia the text catches and communicates to its reader a strange condition: at once excluded and at peace. There can be tranquil moments in the war of languages, and these moments are texts ("War," one of Brecht's characters says, "does not exclude peace . . . War has its peaceful moments . . . Between two skirmishes, there's always time to down a mug of beer . . ."). Between two onslaughts of words, between two imposing systematic presences, the pleasure of the text is always possible, not as a respite, but as the incongruous —dissociated—passage from another language, like the exercise of a different physiology.

Still far too much heroism in our languages; in the best—I am thinking of Bataille's—an erethism of certain expressions and finally a kind of *insidious heroism.* The pleasure of the text (the bliss of the text) is on the contrary like a sudden obliteration of the warrior *value,* a momentary desquamation of the writer's hackles, a suspension of the "heart" (of courage).

How can a text, which consists of language, be outside languages? How *exteriorize* the world's jargons without taking refuge in an ultimate jargon wherein the others would simply be reported, recited? As soon as I name, I am named: caught in the rivalry of names. How can the text "get itself out" of the war of fictions, of sociolects? — by a gradual labor of extenuation. First, the text liquidates all metalanguage, whereby it is text: no voice (Science, Cause, Institution) is *behind* what it is saying. Next, the text destroys utterly, *to the point of contradiction,* its own discursive category, its sociolinguistic reference (its "genre"): it is "the comical that does not make us laugh," the irony which does not subjugate, the jubilation without soul, without mystique (Sarduy), quotation without quotation marks. Lastly, the text can, if it wants, attack the canonical structures of the language itself (Sollers): lexicon (exuberant neologisms, portmanteau words, transliterations), syntax (no more logical cell, no more sentence). It is a matter of effecting, by transmutation (and no longer only by transformation), a new philosophic state of the language-substance; this extraordinary state, this incandescent metal, outside origin and outside communication, then becomes language, and not *a* language, whether disconnected, mimed, mocked.

The pleasure of the text does not prefer one ideology to another. *However:* this impertinence does not proceed from liberalism but from perversion: the text, its reading, are split. What is overcome, split, is the *moral unity* that society demands of every human product. We read a text (of pleasure) the way a fly buzzes around a room: with sudden, deceptively decisive turns, fervent and futile: ideology passes over the text and its reading like the blush over a face (in love, some take erotic pleasure in this coloring); every writer of pleasure has these idiotic blushes (Balzac, Zola, Flaubert, Proust: only Mallarmé, perhaps, is master of his skin): in the text of pleasure, the opposing forces are no longer repressed but in a state of becoming: nothing is really antagonistic, everything is plural. I pass lightly through the reactionary darkness. For example, in

Zola's *Fécondité*, the ideology is flagrant, especially sticky: naturism, family-ism, colonialism; *nonetheless* I continue reading the book. Is such distortion commonplace? Rather, one might be astounded by the housewifely skill with which the subject is meted out, dividing its reading, resisting the contagion of judgment, the metonymy of contentment: can it be that pleasure makes us *objective?*

There are those who want a text (an art, a painting) without a shadow, without the "dominant ideology"; but this is to want a text without fecundity, without productivity, a sterile text (see the myth of the Woman without a Shadow). The text needs its shadow: this shadow is *a bit* of ideology, *a bit* of representation, *a bit* of subject: ghosts, pockets, traces, necessary clouds: subversion must produce its own chiaroscuro.

(Commonly said: "dominant ideology." This expression is incongruous. For what is ideology? It is precisely the idea *insofar as it dominates:* ideology can only be dominant. Correct as it is to speak of an "ideology of the dominant class," because there is certainly a dominated class, it is quite inconsistent to speak of a "dominant ideology," because there is no dominated ideology: where the "dominated" are concerned, there is nothing, no ideology, unless it is precisely—and this is the last degree of alienation—the ideology they are forced (in order to make symbols, hence in order to live) to borrow from the class that dominates them. The social struggle cannot be reduced to the struggle between two rival ideologies: it is the subversion of all ideology which is in question.)

~ ~ ~

To identify accurately language's image-reservoirs, to wit: the word as singular unit, magic monad; speech as instrument or expression of thought; writing as transliteration of speech; the sentence as a logical, closed, measure; the very deficiency or denial of language as a primary, spontaneous, pragmatic force. All these artifacts are governed by the image-reservoir of science (science as image-reservoir): linguistics expresses the truth about language, but solely in this regard: *"that no conscious illusion is perpetrated"*: now, that is the very definition of the image-reservoir: the unconsciousness of the unconscious.

A primary task at the outset is to re-establish within the science of language what is only fortuitously, disdainfully attributed to it, or even more often, rejected: semiology (stylistics, rhetoric, as Nietzsche said), *praxis,* ethical action, "enthusiasm" (Nietzsche again). A second is to restore within science what goes against it: here, the text. The text is language without its image-reservoir, its image-system; it is *what the science of language lacks for its general importance* (and not its technocratic specialization) *to be manifest.* All that is barely tolerated or bluntly rejected by linguistics (as canonical, positive science), significance, bliss—that is precisely what withdraws the text from the image-systems of language.

No "thesis" on the pleasure of the text is possible: barely an inspection (an introspection) that falls short. *Eppure si gaude!* And yet, against and in spite of everything, the text gives me bliss.

At least some examples? One envisions a vast, collective harvest: bring together all the texts *which have given pleasure to someone* (wherever these texts come from) and display this textual body (*corpus:* the right word), in something like the way in which psychoanalysis has exhibited man's erotic body. However, it is to be feared that such a labor would end *explaining* the chosen texts; there would be an inevitable bifurcation of the project: unable to speak itself, pleasure would enter the general path of motivations, *no one of which would be definitive* (if I assert some pleasures of the text here, it is always in passing, in a very precarious, never regular fashion). In short, such a labor could not *be written.* I can only *circle* such a subject—and therefore better to do it briefly and in solitude than collectively and interminably; better to renounce the passage from *value,* the basis of the assertion, to *values,* which are effects of culture.

As a creature of language, the writer is always caught up in the war of fictions (jargons), but he is never anything but a plaything in it, since the language that constitutes him (writing) is always outside-of-place (atopic); by the simple effect of polysemy (rudimentary stage of writing), the warrior commitment of a literary dialect is dubious from its origin. The writer is always on the blind spot of systems, adrift; he is the joker in the pack, a *mana*, a zero degree, the dummy in the bridge game: necessary to the meaning (the battle), but himself deprived of fixed meaning; his place, his (exchange) *value*, varies according to the movements of history, the tactical blows of the struggle: he is asked all and/or nothing. He himself is outside exchange, plunged into non-profit, the Zen *mushotoku*, desiring nothing but the perverse bliss of words (but bliss is never a taking: nothing separates it from *satori*, from losing). Paradox: the writer suppresses this gratuitousness of writing (which approaches, by bliss, the gratuitousness of death): he stiffens, hardens his muscles, denies the drift, represses bliss: there are very few writers who combat *both* ideological repression and libidinal repression (the kind, of course, which the intellectual brings to bear upon himself: upon his own language).

~ ~ ~

Reading a text cited by Stendhal (but not written by him)* I find Proust in one minute detail. The Bishop of Lescars refers to the niece of his vicar-general in a series of affected apostrophes *(My little niece, my little friend, my*

* "Episodes de la vie d'Athanase Auger, publiés par sa nièce," in *Mémoires d'un touriste*, I, pp. 238–245 (Stendhal, *Complete Works*, Calmann-Lévy, 1891).

35

lovely brunette, ah, delicious little morsel!) which remind me
of the way the two post girls at the Grand Hôtel at Balbec,
Marie Geneste and Céleste Albaret, address the narrator
*(Oh, the little black-haired devil, oh, tricky little devil! Ah,
youth! Ah, lovely skin!)*. Elsewhere, but in the same way, in
Flaubert, it is the blossoming apple trees of Normandy
which I read *according to* Proust. I savor the sway of
formulas, the reversal of origins, the ease which brings the
anterior text out of the subsequent one. I recognize that
Proust's work, for myself at least, is *the* reference work, the
general *mathesis,* the *mandala* of the entire literary cos-
mogony—as Mme de Sévigné's letters were for the narrator's grandmother, tales of chivalry for Don Quixote, etc.;
this does not mean that I am in any way a Proust
"specialist": Proust is what comes to me, not what I
summon up; not an "authority," simply a *circular memory.*
Which is what the inter-text is: the impossibility of living
outside the infinite text—whether this text be Proust or the
daily newspaper or the television screen: the book creates
the meaning, the meaning creates life.

~ ~ ~

If you hammer a nail into a piece of wood, the wood has
a different resistance according to the place you attack it:
we say that wood is not isotropic. Neither is the text: the
edges, the seam, are unpredictable. Just as (today's)
physics must accommodate the non-isotropic character of
certain environments, certain universes, so structural anal-

ysis (semiology) must recognize the slightest resistances in the text, the irregular pattern of its veins.

~ ~ ~

No object is in a constant relationship with pleasure (Lacan, apropos of Sade). For the writer, however, this object exists: it is not the language, it is the *mother tongue*. The writer is someone who plays with his mother's body (I refer to Pleynet on Lautréamont and Matisse): in order to glorify it, to embellish it, or in order to dismember it, to take it to the limit of what can be known about the body: I would go so far as to take bliss in a *disfiguration* of the language, and opinion will strenuously object, since it opposes "disfiguring nature."

~ ~ ~

For Bachelard, it seems that writers have never written: by a strange lacuna, they are only read. Thus he has been able to establish a pure critique of reading, and he has grounded it in pleasure: we are engaged in a homogenous (sliding, euphoric, voluptuous, unitary, jubilant) practice, and this practice overwhelms us: *dream-reading*. With Bachelard, it is all poetry (as the simple right to discontinue literature, combat) that is credited to Pleasure. But once the work is perceived in terms of a *writing*, pleasure balks, bliss appears and Bachelard withdraws.

~ ~ ~

I am interested in language because it wounds or seduces me. Can that be a class eroticism? What class? The bourgeoisie? The bourgeoisie has no relish for language, which it no longer regards even as a luxury, an element of the art of living (death of "great" literature), but merely as an instrument of decor (phraseology). The People? Here all magical or poetical activity disappears: the party's over, no more games with words: an end to metaphors, reign of the stereotypes imposed by petit bourgeois culture. (The producing class does not necessarily have the language of its role, of its strength, of its virtue. Thus: dissociation of solidarities, of empathies—powerful here, null there. Critique of the totalizing illusion: any apparatus unifies the language *first,* but one must not respect the whole.)

An islet remains: the text. Delights of caste, mandarinate? pleasure, perhaps; bliss, no.

No significance (no bliss) can occur, I am convinced, in a mass culture (to be distinguished, like fire from water, from the culture of the masses), for the model of this culture is petit bourgeois. It is characteristic of our (historical) contradiction that significance (bliss) has taken refuge in an excessive alternative: either in a mandarin *praxis* (result of an *extenuation* of bourgeois culture), or else in an utopian idea (the idea of a future culture, resulting from a *radical, unheard-of, unpredictable* revolution, about which anyone writing today knows only one thing: that, like Moses, he will not cross over into it).

The asocial character of bliss: it is the abrupt loss of sociality, and yet there follows no recurrence to the subject (subjectivity), the person, solitude: *everything* is lost, integrally. Extremity of the clandestine, darkness of the motion-picture theater.

All socio-ideological analyses agree on the *deceptive* nature of literature (which deprives them of a certain pertinence): the work is finally always written by a socially disappointed or powerless group, beyond the battle because of its historical, economic, political situation; literature is the expression of this disappointment. These analyses forget (which is only normal, since they are hermeneutics based on the exclusive search for the signified) the formidable underside of writing: bliss: bliss which can erupt, across the centuries, out of certain texts that were nonetheless written to the glory of the dreariest, of the most sinister philosophy.

~ ~ ~

The language I speak *within myself* is not of my time; it

is prey, by nature, to ideological suspicion; thus, it is with this language that I must struggle. I write because I do not want the words I find: by subtraction. And at the same time, this *next-to-the-last language* is the language of my pleasure: for hours on end I read Zola, Proust, Verne, *The Count of Monte Cristo*, the *Memoirs of a Tourist*, and sometimes even Julian Green. This is my pleasure, but not my bliss: bliss may come only with the *absolutely new,* for only the new disturbs (weakens) consciousness (easy? not at all: nine times out of ten, the new is only the stereotype of novelty).

The New is not a fashion, it is a value, the basis of all criticism: our evaluation of the world no longer depends, at least not directly, as in Nietzsche, on the opposition between *noble* and *base,* but on that between Old and New (the erotics of the New began in the eighteenth century: a long transformational process). There is only one way left to escape the alienation of present-day society: *to retreat ahead of it:* every old language is immediately compromised, and every language becomes old once it is repeated. Now, encratic language (the language produced and spread under the protection of power) is statutorily a language of repetition; all official institutions of language are repeating machines: school, sports, advertising, popular songs, news, all continually repeat the same structure, the same meaning, often the same words: the stereotype is a political fact, the major figure of ideology. Confronting it, the New is bliss (Freud: "In the adult, novelty always constitutes the condition for orgasm"). Whence the present configuration of forces: on the one hand, a mass banalization (linked to the repetition of language)—a banalization outside bliss but not necessarily outside pleasure—and on the other, a (marginal, eccentric) impulse toward the New—a desperate impulse that can reach the point of destroying discourse: an attempt to reproduce in historical terms the bliss repressed beneath the stereotype.

The opposition (the knife of value) is not necessarily between consecrated, named contraries (materialism and idealism, revolution and reform, etc.); but it is *always and throughout* between the *exception and the rule.* For example, at certain moments it is possible to support the *exception* of the Mystics. Anything, rather than the rule (generality, stereotype, ideolect: the consistent language).

Yet one can make a claim for precisely the opposite (though I am not the one who would make such a claim): repetition itself creates bliss. There are many ethnographic examples: obsessive rhythms, incantatory music, litanies, rites, and Buddhist nembutsu, etc.: to repeat excessively is to enter into loss, into the zero of the signified. But: in order for repetition to be erotic, it must be formal, literal, and in our culture this flaunted (excessive) repetition reverts to eccentricity, thrust toward various marginal regions of music. The bastard form of mass culture is humiliated repetition: content, ideological schema, the blurring of contradictions—these are repeated, but the superficial forms are varied: always new books, new programs, new films, news items, but always the same meaning.

In short, the word can be erotic on two opposing conditions, both excessive: if it is extravagantly repeated, or on the contrary, if it is unexpected, succulent in its newness (in certain texts, words *glisten*, they are distracting, incongruous apparitions—it matters little if they are pedantic; thus, I personally take pleasure in this sentence of Leibnitz: ". . . as though pocket watches told time by means of a certain *horodeictic* faculty, without requiring springs, or as though mills ground grain by means of a *fractive* quality, without requiring anything on the order of millstones"). In both cases, the same physics of bliss, the groove, the inscription, the syncope: what is hollowed out, tamped down, or what explodes, detonates.

The stereotype is the word repeated without any magic, any enthusiasm, as though it were natural, as though by some miracle this recurring word were adequate on each occasion for different reasons, as though to imitate could no longer be sensed as an imitation: an unconstrained word that claims consistency and is unaware of its own insistence. Nietzsche has observed that "truth" is only the solidification of old metaphors. So in this regard the stereotype is the present path of "truth," the palpable feature which shifts the invented ornament to the canonical, constraining form of the signified. (It would be good to imagine a new linguistic science that would no longer study the origin of words, or etymology, or even their diffusion, or lexicology, but the progress of their solidification, their densification throughout historical discourse; this science would doubtless be subversive, manifesting much more than the historical origin of truth: its rhetorical, *languaging* nature.)

The distrust of the stereotype (linked to the bliss of the new word or the untenable discourse) is a principle of absolute instability which respects nothing (no content, no choice). Nausea occurs whenever the liaison of two important words *follows of itself*. And when something follows of itself, I abandon it: that is bliss. A futile annoyance? In Poe's story, M. Valdemar, hypnotized and moribund, is kept alive in a cataleptic state by the repetition of the questions put to him ("Are you asleep, M. Valdemar?"); however, this survival is untenable: the false death, the atrocious death, is what has no end, the interminable. ("For God's sake!—quick!—put me to sleep—or, quick—waken me!—quick!—I say to you that I am dead!") The stereotype is this nauseating impossibility of dying.

In the intellectual field, political choice is a suspension

43

of language—thus a bliss. Yet language resumes, in its consistent stable form (the political stereotype). Which language must then be swallowed, without nausea.

Another bliss (other edges): it consists in de-politicizing what is apparently political, and in politicizing what apparently is not. —Come now, surely one politicizes what *must* be politicized, and that's all.

~ ~ ~

Nihilism: "superior goals depreciate." This is an unstable, jeopardized moment, for other superior values tend, immediately and before the former are destroyed, to prevail; dialectics only links successive positivities; whence the suffocation at the very heart of anarchism. How *install* the deficiency of any superior value? Irony? It always proceeds from a *sure* site. Violence? Violence too is a superior value, and among the best coded. Bliss? Yes, if it is not spoken, doctrinal. The most consistent nihilism is perhaps *masked:* in some way *interior* to institutions, to conformist discourse, to apparent finalities.

~ ~ ~

A. confides that he would not be able to stand his mother's being dissolute—but that he could put up with it in his father; he adds: That's odd, isn't it? —One name would be enough to exorcise his astonishment: *Oedipus!* I regard A. as being very close to the text, for the text *does not give names*—or it removes existing ones; it does not say (or with what *dubious* intent?): Marxism, Brechtism, capitalism, idealism, Zen, etc.; *the Name does not cross its lips,* it is fragmented into practices, into words which are not Names. Bringing itself to the limits of speech, in a *mathesis* of language which does not seek to be identified with science, the text undoes nomination, and it is this defection which approaches bliss.

In an old text I have just read (an episode of ecclesiastical life cited by Stendhal) occurs a naming of foods: milk, buttered bread, cream cheese, preserves, Maltese oranges, sugared strawberries. Is this another pleasure of pure representation (experienced therefore solely by the greedy reader)? But I have no fondness for milk or so many sweets, and I do not project much of myself into the detail of these dishes. Something else occurs, doubtless having to do with another meaning of the word "representation." When, in an argument, someone *represents* something to his interlocutor, he is only allegating the *final state* of reality, its intractability. Similarly, perhaps, the novelist, by citing, naming, *noticing* food (by treating it as notable), imposes on the reader the final state of matter, what cannot be transcended, withdrawn (which is certainly not the case with the nouns cited earlier: *Marxism, idealism,* etc.). *That's it!* This cry is not to be understood as an illumination of the intelligence, but as the very limit of nomination, of the imagination. In short, there are two

45

realisms: the first deciphers the "real" (what is demonstrated but not seen); the second speaks "reality" (what is seen but not demonstrated); the novel, which can mix these two realisms, adds to the intelligible of the "real" the hallucinatory tail of "reality": astonishment that in 1791 one could eat "a salad of oranges and rum," as one does in restaurants today: the onset of historical intelligibility and the persistence of the thing (orange, rum) in *being there*.

~ ~ ~

One out of every two Frenchmen, it appears, does not read; half of France is deprived—deprives itself of the pleasure of the text. Now this national disgrace is never deplored except from a humanistic point of view, as though by ignoring books the French were merely forgoing some moral good, some noble value. It would be better to write the grim, stupid, tragic history of all the pleasures which societies object to or renounce: there is an obscurantism of pleasure.

Even if we shift the pleasure of the text into the field of its theory and not into the field of its sociology (which here entails a particular discourse, apparently void of any national or social meaning), it is still a political alienation which is in question: the foreclosure of pleasure (and even more of bliss) in a society ridden by two moralities: the prevailing one, of platitude; the minority one, of rigor (political and/or scientific). As if the notion of pleasure no longer pleases anyone. Our society appears to be both staid and violent; in any event: frigid.

~ ~ ~

Death of the Father would deprive literature of many of its pleasures. If there is no longer a Father, why tell stories? Doesn't every narrative lead back to Oedipus? Isn't storytelling always a way of searching for one's origin, speaking one's conflicts with the Law, entering into the dialectic of tenderness and hatred? Today, we dismiss Oedipus and narrative at one and the same time: we no longer love, we no longer fear, we no longer narrate. As fiction, Oedipus was at least good for something: to make good novels, to tell good stories (this is written after having seen Murnau's *City Girl*).

Many readings are perverse, implying a split, a cleavage. Just as the child knows its mother has no penis and simultaneously believes she has one (an economy whose validity Freud has demonstrated), so the reader can keep saying: *I know these are only words, but all the same* . . . (I am moved as though these words were uttering a reality). Of all readings, that of tragedy is the most perverse: I take pleasure in hearing myself tell a story *whose end I know:* I know and I don't know, I act toward myself as though I did not know: I know perfectly well Oedipus will be

unmasked, that Danton will be guillotined, *but all the same*
. . . Compared to a dramatic story, which is one whose
outcome is unknown, there is here an effacement of
pleasure and a progression of bliss (today, in mass culture,
there is an enormous consumption of "dramatics" and
little bliss).

~ ~ ~

Proximity (identity?) of bliss and fear. What is repug-
nant in such nearness is obviously not the notion that fear
is a disagreeable feeling—a banal notion—but that it is *not
a very worthy feeling;* fear is the misfit of every philosophy
(except, I believe, Hobbes's remark that the one passion of
his life had been fear); madness wants nothing to do with
it (except perhaps old-fashioned madness: Maupassant's
Horla), and this keeps fear from being modern: it is a
denial of transgression, a madness which you leave off in
full consciousness. By a last fatality, the subject who
suffers fear still remains a subject; at most, he is answera-
ble to neurosis (we then speak of *anxiety,* a noble word, a
scientific word: but fear is not anxiety).

These are the very reasons which unite fear and bliss:
fear is absolute clandestinity, not because it is "unavowa-
ble" (although today no one is willing to avow it), but
because, splitting the subject *while leaving him intact,* it can
wield only *conforming* signifiers: the language of madness
is not available to a man listening to fear rising within
himself. *"I write not to be mad,"* Bataille said—which

meant that he wrote madness; but which could mean: "*I write not to be afraid*"? Who could write fear (which would not mean, tell about it)? Fear does not pursue, nor does it constrain, nor does it accomplish writing: by the stubbornest of contradictions, both coexist—separated. (Not to mention the case in which *to write makes one afraid*.)

~ ~ ~

One evening, half asleep on a banquette in a bar, just for fun I tried to enumerate all the languages within earshot: music, conversations, the sounds of chairs, glasses, a whole stereophony of which a square in Tangiers (as described by Severo Sarduy) is the exemplary site. That too spoke within me, and this so-called "interior" speech was very like the noise of the square, like that amassing of minor voices coming to me from the outside: I myself was a public square, a _sook;_ through me passed words, tiny syntagms, bits of formulae, and *no sentence formed,* as though that were the law of such a language. This speech, at once very cultural and very savage, was above all lexical, sporadic; it set up in me, through its apparent flow, a definitive discontinuity: this *non-sentence* was in no way something that could not have acceded to the sentence, that might have been *before* the sentence; it was: what is eternally, splendidly, *outside the sentence.* Then, potentially, all linguistics fell, linguistics which believes only in the sentence and has always attributed an exorbitant dignity to predicative syntax (as the form of a logic, of a rationality); I recalled this scientific scandal: there exists no locutive grammar (a grammar of what is spoken and not of what is written; and to begin with: a grammar of spoken French). We are delivered to the sentence, to the *phrase,* as we call it in French (and hence: to phraseology).

The Sentence is hierarchical: it implies subjections, subordinations, internal reactions. Whence its completion: how can a hierarchy remain open? The Sentence is complete: it is even precisely that language which is complete. Practice, here, is very different from theory. Theory (Chomsky) says that the sentence is potentially infinite (infinitely catalyzable), but practice always obliges the sentence to end. "Every ideological activity is presented in the form of compositionally completed utterances." Let us also take Julia Kristeva's proposition in reverse: any completed utterance runs the risk of being ideological. In fact, it is the power of completion which defines sentence mastery and marks, as with a supreme, dearly won, conquered *savoir-faire,* the agents of the Sentence. The professor is someone who finishes his sentences. The politician being interviewed clearly takes a great deal of trouble to imagine an ending to his sentence: and if he stopped short? His entire policy would be jeopardized! And the writer? Valéry said: "One does not think words, one thinks only sentences." He said it because he was a writer. A writer is not someone who expresses his thoughts, his passion, or his imagination in sentences, but *someone who thinks sentences:* A Sentence-Thinker (i.e., not altogether a thinker and not altogether a sentence-parser).

The pleasure of the sentence is to a high degree cultural. The artifact created by rhetors, grammarians, linguists, teachers, writers, parents—this artifact is mimicked in a more or less ludic manner; we are playing with an exceptional object, whose paradox has been articulated by linguistics: immutably structured and yet infinitely renewable: something like chess.

Unless for some perverts the sentence is a *body?*

~ ~ ~

Pleasure of the text. Classics. Culture (the more culture, the greater, more diverse, the pleasure will be). Intelligence. Irony. Delicacy. Euphoria. Mastery. Security: art of living. The pleasure of the text can be defined by *praxis* (without any danger of repression): the time and place of reading: house, countryside, near mealtime, the lamp, family where it should be, i.e., close but not too close (Proust in the lavatory that smelled of orrisroot), etc. Extraordinary ego-reinforcement (by fantasy), the unconscious muffled. This pleasure can be *spoken:* whence criticism.

Texts of pleasure. Pleasure in pieces; language in pieces; culture in pieces. Such texts are perverse in that they are outside any imaginable finality—*even that of pleasure* (bliss does not constrain to pleasure; it can even apparently inflict boredom). No alibi stands up, nothing is reconstituted, nothing recuperated. The text of bliss is absolutely intransitive. However, perversion does not suffice to define bliss; it is the extreme of perversion which defines it: an extreme continually shifted, an empty, mobile, unpredictable extreme. This extreme guarantees bliss: an average perversion quickly loads itself up with a play of subordinate finalities: prestige, ostentation, rivalry, lecturing, self-serving, etc.

Everyone can testify that the pleasure of the text is not certain: nothing says that this same text will please us a second time; it is a friable pleasure, split by mood, habit, circumstance, a precarious pleasure (obtained by a silent prayer addressed to the Desire for ease, and which that Desire can revoke); whence the impossibility of speaking about this text from the point of view of positive science (its jurisdiction is that of critical science: pleasure is a critical principle).

The bliss of the text is not precarious, it is worse: *precocious;* it does not come in its own good time, it does not depend on any ripening. Everything is wrought to a transport at one and the same moment. This transport is evident in painting, today's painting: as soon as it is understood, the principle of loss becomes ineffective, one must go on to something else. Everything comes about; indeed in every sense everything *comes—at first glance.*

~ ~ ~

The text is (should be) that uninhibited person who shows his behind to the *Political Father.*

~ ~ ~

Why do some people, including myself, enjoy in certain novels, biographies, and historical works the representation of the "daily life" of an epoch, of a character? Why this curiosity about petty details: schedules, habits, meals, lodging, clothing, etc.? Is it the hallucinatory relish of "reality" (the very materiality of *"that once existed"*)? And is it not the fantasy itself which invokes the "detail," the tiny private scene, in which I can easily take my place? Are there, in short, "minor hysterics" (these very readers) who receive bliss from a singular theater: not one of grandeur but one of mediocrity (might there not be dreams, fantasies of mediocrity)?

Thus, impossible to imagine a more tenuous, a more insignificant notation than that of "today's weather" (or yesterday's); and yet, the other day, reading, trying to read Amiel, irritation that the well-meaning editor (another person foreclosing pleasure) had seen fit to omit from this Journal the everyday details, what the weather was like on

53

the shores of Lake Geneva, and retain only insipid moral musing: yet it is this weather that has not aged, not Amiel's philosophy.

~ ~ ~

Art seems compromised, historically, socially. Whence the effort on the part of the artist himself to destroy it.

I see this effort taking three forms. The artist can shift to another signifier: if he is a writer, he becomes a film-maker, a painter, or, contrariwise, if he is a painter, a film-maker, he works up interminable critiques of the cinema, painting, deliberately reduces the art to his criticism. He can also "dismiss" writing and become a scientist, a scholar, an intellectual theorist, no longer speaking except from a moral site cleansed of any linguistic sensuality. Finally, he can purely and simply scuttle himself, stop writing, change trades, change desires.

Unfortunately, this destr.ction is always inadequate; either it occurs outside the art, but thereby becomes impertinent, or else it consents to remain within the practice of the art, but quickly exposes itself to recuperation (the avant-garde is that restive language which is going to be recuperated). The awkwardness of this alternative is the consequence of the fact that destruction of discourse is not a dialectic term *but a semantic term:* it docilely takes its place within the great semiological "versus" myth (*white* versus *black*); whence the destruction of art is doomed to only *paradoxical* formulae (those which proceed literally against the *doxa*): both sides of the paradigm are glued together in an ultimately complicitous fashion: there is a structural agreement between the contesting and the contested forms.

(By *subtle subversion* I mean, on the contrary, what is not directly concerned with destruction, evades the paradigm, and seeks some *other* term: a third term, which is not, however, a synthesizing term but an eccentric, extraordinary term. An example? Perhaps Bataille, who eludes the idealist term by an *unexpected* materialism in which we find vice, devotion, play, impossible eroticism, etc.; thus Bataille does not counter modesty with sexual freedom but . . . with *laughter*.)

~ ~ ~

The text of pleasure is not necessarily the text that recounts pleasures; the text of bliss is never the text that recounts the kind of bliss afforded literally by an ejaculation. The pleasure of representation is not attached to its object: pornography is not *sure*. In zoological terms, one could say that the site of textual pleasure is not the relation of mimic and model (imitative relation) but solely that of dupe and mimic (relation of desire, of production).

We must, moreover, distinguish between *figuration* and *representation*.

Figuration is the way in which the erotic body appears

(to whatever degree and in whatever form that may be) in the profile of the text. For example: the author may appear in his text (Genet, Proust), but not in the guise of direct biography (which would exceed the body, give a meaning to life, forge a destiny). Or again: one can feel desire for a character in a novel (in fleeting impulses). Or finally: the text itself, a diagrammatic and not an imitative structure, can reveal itself in the form of a body, split into fetish objects, into erotic sites. All these movements attest to a *figure* of the text, necessary to the bliss of reading. Similarly, and even more than the text, the film will *always* be figurative (which is why films are still worth making)— even if it represents nothing.

Representation, on the other hand, is *embarrassed figuration,* encumbered with other meanings than that of desire: a space of alibis (reality, morality, likelihood, readability, truth, etc.). Here is a text of pure representation: Barbey d'Aurevilly writes on Memling's Virgin: "She stands upright, very perpendicularly posed. Pure beings are upright. By posture and by movement, we know the chaste woman; wantons droop, languish and lean, always about to fall." Note in passing that the representative undertaking has managed to engender an art (the classical novel) as well as a "science" (graphology, for example, which deduces from the attenuation of a single letter the listlessness of the writer), and that it is consequently fair, without any sophistry, to call it immediately ideological (by the historical extent of its signification). Of course, it very often happens that representation takes desire itself as an object of imitation; but then, such desire never leaves the frame, the picture; it circulates among the characters; if it has a recipient, that recipient remains interior to the fiction (consequently, we can say that any semiotics that keeps desire within the configuration of those upon whom it acts, however new it may be, is a semiotics of representation. That is what representation is: when nothing emerges, when nothing leaps out of the frame: of the picture, the book, the screen).

~ ~ ~

No sooner has a word been said, somewhere, about the pleasure of the text, than two policemen are ready to jump on you: the political policeman and the psychoanalytical policeman: futility and/or guilt, pleasure is either idle or vain, a class notion or an illusion.

An old, a very old tradition: hedonism has been repressed by nearly every philosophy; we find it defended only by marginal figures, Sade, Fourier; for Nietzsche, hedonism is a pessimism. Pleasure is continually disappointed, reduced, deflated, in favor of strong, noble values: Truth, Death, Progress, Struggle, Joy, etc. Its victorious rival is Desire: we are always being told about Desire, never about Pleasure; Desire has an epistemic dignity, Pleasure does not. It seems that (our) society refuses (and ends up by ignoring) bliss to such a point that it can produce only epistemologies of the law (and of its contestation), never of its absence, or better still: of its nullity. Odd, this philosophical permanence of Desire (insofar as it is never satisfied): doesn't the word itself denote a "class notion"? (A rather crude presumption of proof, and yet noteworthy: the "populace" does not know Desire—only pleasures.)

So-called "erotic" books (one must add: of recent vintage, in order to except Sade and a few others) *represent* not so much the erotic scene as the expectation of it, the preparation for it, its ascent; that is what makes them "exciting"; and when the scene occurs, naturally there is disappointment, deflation. In other words, these are books of Desire, not of Pleasure. Or, more mischievously, they represent Pleasure *as seen by psychoanalysis*. A like meaning says, in both instances, that *the whole thing is very disappointing*.

(The monument of psychoanalysis must be traversed—not bypassed—like the fine thoroughfares of a very large city, across which we can play, dream, etc.: a fiction.)

There is supposed to be a mystique of the Text. —On the contrary, the whole effort consists in materializing the pleasure of the text, in making the text *an object of pleasure like the others*. That is: either relate the text to the "pleasures" of life (a dish, a garden, an encounter, a voice, a moment, etc.) and to it join the personal catalogue of our sensualities, or force the text to breach bliss, that immense subjective loss, thereby identifying this text with the purest moments of perversion, with its clandestine sites. The important thing is to equalize the field of pleasure, to abolish the false opposition of practical life and contemplative life. The pleasure of the text is just that: claim lodged against the separation of the text; for what the text says, through the particularity of its name, is the ubiquity of pleasure, the atopia of bliss.

Notion of a book (of a text) in which is braided, woven, in the most personal way, the relation of every kind of bliss: those of "life" and those of the text, in which reading and the risks of real life are subject to the same anamnesis.

Imagine an aesthetic (if the word has not become too depreciated) based entirely (completely, radically, in every sense of the word) on the *pleasure of the consumer,* whoever he may be, to whatever class, whatever group he may belong, without respect to cultures or languages: the consequences would be huge, perhaps even harrowing (Brecht has sketched such an aesthetic of pleasure; of all his proposals, this is the one most frequently forgotten).

~ ~ ~

Dreaming allows for, supports, releases, brings to light an extreme delicacy of moral, sometimes even metaphysical, sentiments, the subtlest sense of human relations, refined differences, a learning of the highest civilization, in short a conscious logic, articulated with an extraordinary finesse, which only an intense waking labor would be able to achieve. In short, dreaming makes *everything in me which is not strange, foreign,* speak: the dream is an uncivil anecdote made up of very civilized sentiments (the dream is *civilizing*).

The text of bliss often stages this differential (Poe); but it can also produce the contrary figure (albeit just as divided): a very readable anecdote with *impossible* sentiments (Bataille's *Mme Edwarda*).

~ ~ ~

What relation can there be between the pleasure of the text and the institutions of the text? Very slight. The theory of the text postulates bliss, but it has little institutional future: what it establishes, its precise accomplishment, its assumption, is a practice (that of the writer), not a science, a method, a research, a pedagogy; on these very principles, this theory can produce only theoreticians or practitioners, not specialists (critics, researchers, professors, students). It is not only the inevitably metalinguistic nature of all institutional research which hampers the writing of textual pleasure, it is also that we are today incapable of conceiving a true science of becoming (which alone might assemble our pleasure without garnishing it with a moral tutelage): "We are not *subtle* enough to perceive that probably *absolute flow of becoming;* the *permanent* exists only thanks to our coarse organs which reduce and lead things to shared premises of vulgarity, whereas nothing exists *in this form.* A tree is a new thing at every instant; we affirm the *form* because we do not seize the subtlety of an absolute moment" (Nietzsche).

The Text too is this tree whose (provisional) nomination we owe to the coarseness of our organs. We are scientific because we lack subtlety.

~ ~ ~

What is significance? It is meaning, *insofar as it is sensually produced.*

~ ~ ~

What we are seeking to establish in various ways is a theory of the materialist subject. This undertaking can pass through three stages: first, taking an old psychological path, it can relentlessly criticize the illusions the imaginary subject surrounds itself with (classical moralists have excelled in this sort of criticism); next—or simultaneously—it can go further, acknowledge the dizzying schism in the subject, described as a pure alternation, the alternation of zero and of its effacement (this concerns the text, since, though incapable of being *spoken* there, bliss nonetheless transmits the shudder of its annihilation); finally, it can generalize the subject ("multiple soul," "moral soul")—which does not mean collectivize it; and here again, we come back to the text, pleasure, bliss. "We have no right to ask *who* it is who interprets. It is interpretation itself, a form of the will to power, which exists (not as 'being' but as process, a becoming) as passion" (Nietzsche).

Then perhaps the subject returns, not as illusion, but as *fiction*. A certain pleasure is derived from a way of imagining oneself as *individual*, of inventing a final, rarest fiction: the fictive identity. This fiction is no longer the illusion of a unity; on the contrary, it is the theater of society in which we stage our plural: our pleasure is *individual*—but not personal.

Whenever I attempt to "analyze" a text which has given me pleasure, it is not my "subjectivity" I encounter but my "individuality," the given which makes my body separate from other bodies and appropriates its suffering or its pleasure: it is my body of bliss I encounter. And this body of bliss is also *my historical subject;* for it is at the conclusion of a very complex process of biographical, historical, sociological, neurotic elements (education, so-cial class, childhood configuration, etc.) that I control the contradictory interplay of (cultural) pleasure and (non-cultural) bliss, and that I write myself as a subject at present out of place, arriving too soon or too late (this *too* designating neither regret, fault, nor bad luck, but merely calling for a *non-site*): anachronic subject, adrift.

We can imagine a typology of the pleasures of reading —or of the readers of pleasure; it would not be sociological, for pleasure is not an attribute of either product or production; it could only be psychoanalytic, linking the reading neurosis to the hallucinated form of the text. The fetishist would be matched with the divided-up text, the singling out of quotations, formulae, turns of phrase, with the pleasure of the word. The obsessive would experience the voluptuous release of the letter, of secondary, disconnected languages, of metalanguages (this class would include all the logophiles, linguists, semioticians, philologists: all those for whom language *returns*). A paranoiac would consume or produce complicated texts, stories developed like arguments, constructions posited like games, like secret constraints. As for the hysteric (so contrary to the obsessive), he would be the one who takes the text *for ready money,* who joins in the bottomless, truthless comedy of language, who is no longer the subject of any critical scrutiny and *throws himself* across the text (which is quite different from projecting himself into it).

~ ~ ~

Text means *Tissue;* but whereas hitherto we have always taken this tissue as a product, a ready-made veil, behind which lies, more or less hidden, meaning (truth), we are now emphasizing, in the tissue, the generative idea that the text is made, is worked out in a perpetual interweaving; lost in this tissue—this texture—the subject unmakes himself, like a spider dissolving in the constructive secretions of its web. Were we fond of neologisms, we might define the theory of the text as an *hyphology* (*hyphos* is the tissue and the spider's web).

Although the theory of the text has specifically designated significance (in the sense Julia Kristeva has given this word) as the site of bliss, although it has affirmed the simultaneously erotic and critical value of textual practice, these propositions are often forgotten, repressed, stifled. And yet: is the radical materialism this theory tends toward conceivable without the notions of pleasure, of bliss? Have not the rare materialists of the past, each in his way, Epicurus, Diderot, Sade, Fourier, all been overt eudaemonists?

Yet the position of pleasure in a theory of the text is not certain. Simply, a day comes when we feel a certain need to *loosen* the theory a bit, to shift the discourse, the ideolect which repeats itself, becomes consistent, and to give it the shock of a question. Pleasure is this question. As a trivial, unworthy name (who today would call himself a hedonist with a straight face?), it can embarrass the text's return to morality, to truth: to the morality of truth: it is an oblique, a drag anchor, so to speak, without which the theory of the text would revert to a centered system, a philosophy of meaning.

~ ~ ~

Pleasure's force of *suspension* can never be overstated: it is a veritable *époché*, a stoppage which congeals all recognized values (recognized by oneself). Pleasure is a *neuter* (the most perverse form of the demoniac).

Or at least, what pleasure suspends is the *signified* value: the (good) cause. "Darmès, a scribbler who is on trial at the moment for having shot at the king, is preparing his political ideas for publication . . . ; what Darmès writes about most frequently is the aristocracy, which he spells *'haristokrassy.'* The word, written this way, is terrible indeed . . ." Hugo *(Pierres)* has an acute appreciation of the extravagance of the signifier; he also knows that this little orthographic orgasm comes from Darmès's "ideas": his ideas, i.e., his values, his political belief, the evaluation that makes him in a single moment write, name, misspell, and spew up. Yet: how boring Darmés's political pamphlet must have been! That is the pleasure of the text: value shifted to the sumptuous rank of the signifier.

~ ~ ~

If it were possible to imagine an aesthetic of textual pleasure, it would have to include: *writing aloud.* This vocal writing (which is nothing like speech) is not practiced, but it is doubtless what Artaud recommended and what Sollers is demanding. Let us talk about it as though it existed.

In antiquity, rhetoric included a section which is forgotten, censored by classical commentators: the *actio,* a group of formulae designed to allow for the corporeal exteriorization of discourse: it dealt with a theater of expression, the actor-orator "expressing" his indignation, his compassion, etc. *Writing aloud* is not expressive; it leaves expression to the pheno-text, to the regular code of communication; it belongs to the geno-text, to significance; it is carried not by dramatic inflections, subtle stresses, sympathetic accents, but by the *grain* of the voice, which is an erotic mixture of timbre and language, and can therefore also be, along with diction, the substance of an art: the art of guiding one's body (whence its importance in Far Eastern theaters). Due allowance being made for the sounds of the language, *writing aloud* is not phonological but phonetic; its aim is not the clarity of messages, the theater of emotions; what it searches for (in a perspective of bliss) are the pulsional incidents, the language lined with flesh, a text where we can hear the grain of the throat, the patina of consonants, the voluptuousness of vowels, a whole carnal stereophony: the articulation of the body, of

66

the tongue, not that of meaning, of language. A certain art of singing can give an idea of this vocal writing; but since melody is dead, we may find it more easily today at the cinema. In fact, it suffices that the cinema capture the sound of speech *close up* (this is, in fact, the generalized definition of the "grain" of writing) and make us hear in their materiality, their sensuality, the breath, the gutturals, the fleshiness of the lips, a whole presence of the human muzzle (that the voice, that writing, be as fresh, supple, lubricated, delicately granular and vibrant as an animal's muzzle), to succeed in shifting the signified a great distance and in throwing, so to speak, the anonymous body of the actor into my ear: it granulates, it crackles, it caresses, it grates, it cuts, it comes: that is bliss.